THE
FITNESS FAMILY
COOKBOOK

By Sophie Watkins & Jordan Storey

Dedication

We are dedicating this book to the next generation.

To help encourage and educate others on the importance of a healthy balanced lifestyle, and together bring down the ever-growing statistics of high blood pressure, heart attacks, and diabetes.

Contents

1

INTRODUCTION

INTRODUCTION

Our family cookbook is as much about having fun as creating a healthy lifestyle.

There are different recipe ideas and fun activities for all to enjoy with top tips for parents and educational facts for kids.

With Jordan's expertise in nutrition and my passion for a healthy family lifestyle, we have combined our knowledge to create the perfect recipe book for all to use. We both feel so strongly about the ever-growing obesity charts for children, and we hope to tackle and decrease those stats.

Our traffic-light colour-coding scheme makes it much easier to pair together meals, especially if you are watching those waistlines. We've included the full nutritional values for each meal, and some top tips and educational but fun facts. It's great to eat a healthy meal, it's even better to be able to see exactly what you are putting into your own body, and more importantly, your children's bodies.

We've also added in some bulk cook recipes, making easy on-the-go meals for busy schedules and we have also included family activities and sit-down dinner meals. This book has a bit of everything, and we have tried to cater for families of all kinds.

We hope you use this book and take away with you a fresh approach to healthy eating. People can assume that healthy eating is expensive, boring, and repetitive, but we have included a wide cost-effective variety of meals to steer away from this stereotype.

We'd both love to hear from you on how you are getting on – check out our social media contact information at the end of this book.

We hope you enjoy using this book, as much as we did creating it.

Sophie and Jordan xx

About Sophie ...

When Jordan first approached me with the idea to combine our passions to create the perfect family recipe book, I was immediately excited by the idea. As a busy mum of three boys, I've tried to find this exact book in the past and failed, so it left me with no choice but to agree and add 'author' to my never-ending list of job titles, as us mums do.

My husband Kallum is a sportsman. He is the ultimate professional, and on top of his extensive training routine, he's very passionate about what he puts into his body; a quality I would love to pass down to our boys. A healthy lifestyle is very important for both the physical and mental aspects of our lives. A gym workout, followed by a healthy dinner is the perfect recipe for a happy home.

I am not claiming to be a 'Zen' mum. I am the occasional chicken nugget and chips drive-thru mum, but what I am passionate about is everything in moderation. The recipes in this book will give you a fun approach to healthy eating, with a few fun tips and facts thrown in. In the past, I've been known to tell my children, "oh no, you won't like that," without even realising that I was contributing to a bad relationship with food.

I now encourage my children to at least try everything, and by involving them in family cooking activities, it makes the whole process much more rewarding.

With love …

Sophie Watkins xx

About Jordan ...

I've been in the fitness industry now for over 12 years, and I've worked with all types of people from all aspects of life; from your average Joe to professional sports people & TV celebrities.

My true passion though comes from helping the public achieve their personal goals and watching them grow physically but most importantly, mentally as well. Fitness can give you a great boost in confidence and heighten your mood and outlook on life.

I am a fully qualified nutritionist and personal trainer, and I am continually looking at ways of improving my own knowledge through experience so I can provide a better service to all my clients.

The idea came to me having worked with many mothers and fathers who always seemed to struggle with meal ideas for their families. I was being asked more and more about involving the whole family when it came to healthy meal plans, so I decided to approach Sophie (a busy mum with three young boys) with the idea for this book.

I've written hundreds of personal diets for my clients and witnessed the amazing results that they can achieve. I wanted to be able to make an even bigger impact for those that I couldn't see on a one-to-one basis. I've created this cookbook with Sophie so that it would reach out to an even bigger audience.

We all know that following a poor diet is bad for you, not only when it comes to a person's physical appearance and health, but also for their mental wellbeing. Studies show that a healthy approach has also helped many mental disorders such as depression. I have been witness to this time and again.

It's easy to fall into bad habits and find yourself in a 'rut' and then before you know it you've gained excessive weight, which impacts on all areas of your life. It can lower your confidence and make socialising and going out to social events far less enjoyable.

I hope that this book will encourage you to vary your culinary repertoire. Please have fun making these great, easy, and nutritious laden meals with your family, and enjoy all the benefits that come with this new approach to mealtime.

Enjoy!

Jordan xx

Meal Prep

Cooking more meals at home is far more healthy as you know exactly what is going into your food. It can also be a lot healthier for your shopping budget.

It's all about planning, but this need not be time-consuming, even for the busiest of people. The plan is to spend as little time in the kitchen as you have to by being prepared.

A great way to do this is by making a list of all the meals you are going to have for the week ahead. Choose one recipe each from our Breakfast, Lunch, and Dinner menus per day, but make sure if watching your waistline is high on your agenda that you do not choose all RED meals!

Choose specific menus that you will all enjoy – perhaps do the planning with the kids, so they feel a part of the process. Children also like knowing what to expect, and you are less likely to get moans and groans about all the healthy options we've created if they're involved from the outset.

Please note: There's a difference between uncooked and cooked weight – the uncooked weight is better as it reduces waste.

Our Lazy Spice List

These are cupboard essentials and will help to keep you on track.

Healthy eating doesn't have to be tasteless and boring!

So make sure you have the following …

Garlic, chili, ginger, paprika, cinnamon, cumin, garam masala and bake in the bags.

Our Super Sauce List

The best options to use are …

Soy, 50% reduced sugar and salt ketchup, brown sauce, teriyaki, lighter than light mayo, mustard, red hot sauce, and peri peri sauce.

2

BREAKFAST

Parents and kids
120g of porridge oats
500ml of unsweetened
coconut milk
2 bananas
2 tbsp honey (replace with
maple syrup for vegan option)

Goldilock's Porridge

Let's get microwaving!

Mix the porridge oats, milk or water in a large microwave proof bowl, then microwave on High for 5 minutes, stirring halfway through. Leave to stand for 2 minutes before eating.

Whilst waiting for the porridge to cool, chop the banana into small chunks.

To serve, pour into bowls, add the banana on top, and drizzle with honey.

FUN FACT PARENTS
- your porridge shouldn't be too hot or too cold.

FUN FACT KIDS
- yours will be just right.

Nutritional value
Calories 202
Protein 4.5g
Carbs 38g
Fats 3g

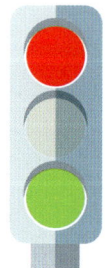

Parents and kids

3 bananas
150g porridge oats
½ tsp cinnamon
200ml unsweetened almond
milk (plus extra
to serve)
2tbsp cocoa powder
6 chopped walnuts

Baked Chocolate & Banana Porridge

Let's get baking!

Heat the oven to 190C/170C fan/gas 5. Mash up one banana half, then mix it with the oats, cinnamon, cocoa powder, milk, 300ml water and a pinch of salt.

Pour the mixture into a baking dish.

Top with the remaining banana halves, and scatter over the walnuts.

Bake for 20-25 minutes until the oats are creamy and have absorbed most of the liquid.

Add extra milk to serve, and enjoy!

TOP TIP PARENTS AND KIDS
- add a few chocolate sprinkles, for a special weekend treat.

Nutritional value
Calories 200
Protein 8g
Carbs 42g
Fats 5g

Breakfast Smoothie

Parents
80g porridge oats
2 scoops whey protein
1 banana
40g organic peanut butter
500ml unsweetened almond milk

Kids
40g porridge oats
1 banana
100g mixed berries
30g peanut butter
500ml oat milk

Let's get blending!

Kids, this one is for you! Help your grown-up gather and weigh out all of the ingredients.

Grown-ups, throw the kid's ingredients into the blending cup, whizz it up for 20 seconds, and watch a healthy breakfast smoothie evolve.

Repeat this with your own ingredients. Yes, we know, kids are like customers- they always come first!

Divide it between your glasses and enjoy!

TOP TIP PARENTS
- To kick start your day, add two heaps of coffee granules to your smoothie.

TOP TIP KIDS
- South Americans were the first to introduce smoothies, and they called it the fruit slush.

Nutritional value
Calories 492
Protein 35g
Carbs 42g
Fats 15g

Buckwheat and Blueberry Jam Pancakes

Parents and kids

100g buckwheat flour
1 ½ tsp baking powder
2 eggs
100 ml milk of your choice
120g blueberries
Agave or maple syrup

Let's get cooking!

Whisk the eggs and milk together in a jug. Sieve the flour into a mixing bowl and add the baking powder. Gradually add the wet ingredients to the dry and whisk. Add a pinch of salt and leave to rest for 1 hour.

Heat a spray of oil in a frying pan on a medium heat. Add a large spoonful of batter to the pan, and make a pancake. Once golden, flip the pancake over. Repeat with the remaining batter.

Add the blueberries to the pan for 2 minutes, and mash with a fork to create the jam.

Put the pancakes onto plates, top with the jam, and finish with a drizzle of syrup.

TOP TIP PARENTS
- to make the pancakes 100% percent vegan, use 6g of egg replacer, with 4 tbsp of water.

TOP TIP KIDS
- test out different fruit toppers to find your favourite pancake combination.

Nutritional value

Calories 190
Protein 8g
Carbs 27g
Fats 5g

Parents and kids

150g oatmeal
2 bananas
40 g raisins
600ml of coconut milk
2 tbsp maple syrup
4 tsp almond butter (topper)
Coconut shavings

Coconut and Banana Oatmeal

Let's get cooking!

Combine oatmeal, bananas, raisins, coconut milk and maple syrup in a pan.

Bring to a boil over medium heat. Once boiling, stir only occasionally to prevent sticking or boiling over.

It will eventually thicken. Divide between bowls and top with almond butter and coconut shavings.

TOP TIP PARENTS
- Serve hot, or refrigerate overnight and serve either hot or cold the next day.

FUN FACT KIDS
- The 29th of October is National Oatmeal Day in the USA.

Nutritional value
Calories 339
Protein 10g
Carbs 48g
Fats 13g

Overnight Oats

Let's get prepping!

Parents
1/2 tsp ground cinnamon
100g rolled porridge oats
4 tbsp natural yogurt
100g mixed berries
240ml oat milk
drizzle of honey
1 tbsp nut butter (we love almond)

Kids
50g oats
2 tbsp natural yoghurt
1 banana
120ml oat milk
Drizzle of honey
Sprinkle of chocolate chips

Add the rolled oats to a container of your choice and pour over the milk.

Layer the yoghurt, fruit, and nut butter (or chocolate chips for the kids), then refrigerate overnight to enjoy in the morning.

TOP TIP PARENTS
- when kept in an airtight container, overnight oats can last in the fridge for up to 5 days!

TOP TIP KIDS
- swap the honey to maple syrup for an extra tasty treat.

Nutritional value
Calories 310
Protein 12g
Carbs 35g
Fats 11g

Parents and kids

6 slices of thick cut whole grain bread
4 large eggs
6 slices of bacon
250ml of unsweetened almond milk
150ml of fresh orange juice
1 tsp vanilla extract
1 tsp cinnamon
¼ nutmeg
1 tbsp maple syrup (plus more for topping)

French Toast with Bacon

Let's get cooking!

Kids! In a large bowl whisk together eggs, almond milk, orange juice, vanilla, cinnamon, nutmeg, and maple syrup.

Place half of the mixture into a shallow dish. Add 3 bread slices at a time, and allow to soak for 2 minutes on each side.

Grown-ups! Heat two pans.

Throw the bacon rashers in one pan, and cook the bread on each side for 3-4 minutes in the other pan.

Repeat with the remaining slices and egg mixture, and once cooked, remove the bacon from the pan.

Serve the french toast up, and add the bacon and syrup topping.

TOP TIP PARENTS AND KIDS
- swap maple syrup for honey if you prefer it, they have around the same nutritional value.

Nutritional value
Calories 402
Protein 19g
Carbs 37g
Fats 18g

Parents

1 avocado
2 chunks of sourdough bread
4 eggs
25g Feta cheese
½ Lemon
½ tsp chili flakes

Kids

1 avocado (use butter as
substitute)
2 chunks of sourdough bread
2 eggs
Squirt of low salt tomato
sauce

Avo on Toast with Eggs

Let's get cooking!

To get started prep your avocado, take a sharp knife and chop it in half taking extra care of the stone in the middle. Remove the stone and spoon out the avocado into a bowl. Using a fork, mash the avocado, creating a chunky texture.

Grown-ups, set aside the little one's share, and sprinkle the chili flakes into your portion. Finish off the mash with a little squeeze of lemon.

Pre-cut your sourdough slabs, ready to stick in the toaster later on.

Eggs! Bring a deep pan of water to boil, (add a pinch of salt). Crack the egg straight into the water, and leave to cook for 3-4 minutes.

Toast the sourdough whilst the eggs are cooking.

TOP TIP PARENTS
- add salmon for something a little more special.

TOP TIP KIDS
- try the eggs scrambled instead of poached.

Nutritional value
Calories 425
Protein 20g
Carbs 22.5g
Fats 28.5g

Spread the avocado mash, over the toasted sourdough. Pull the eggs out of the pan using a slotted spoon, and place carefully on top. You should have a perfectly runny poached egg, don't worry if not- you'll be eggcellent after a little bit of practice.

If you're a feta fan, finish with a cheese topping. For the little ones, add a splash of red sauce.

Parents

4 eggs
4 slices of oven baked ham
Handful of chestnut mushrooms
Handful of Cherry tomatoes
Handful of spinach

Kids

2 eggs
2 slices of oven baked ham
Handful of chestnut mushrooms
Handful of Cherry tomatoes
Handful of spinach

Fried Eggs with Ham

Let's get cooking!

Grown-ups, heat two pans with a spritz or two of fry light. Place the ham slices into one pan, and turn them over after a minute, just long enough to heat them through.

Throw the mushrooms, tomatoes, and spinach into the other heated pan, and leave them to cook.

Break an egg into a ramekin, then carefully slide the egg on top of the ham.

Repeat this with the other eggs and ham slices.

Cook until the eggs are done as you like them, we recommend around three minutes for a runny yolk.

Slide a spatula under the egg and ham slices, and place onto a plate. Top with the mushrooms, spinach, and tomatoes.

TOP TIP PARENTS
- add chili flakes for a little kick.

TOP TIP KIDS
- if a fried egg isn't your thing, try poached instead.

Nutritional value
Calories 300
Protein 35g
Carbs 2g
Fat 13g

Acai Bowl

Parents and kids

400ml of apple juice
2 large bananas, sliced
200g of frozen berries
120g vanilla Greek yogurt
2 tablespoons of honey
2 frozen packet of acai berry
puree (100 grams), broken
into pieces.

Assorted toppings such as
sliced almonds, berries,
shredded coconut, granola,
chia seeds, sliced banana,
mint sprigs, etc.

Let's get prepping!

Place the apple juice, banana, frozen berries, yogurt, honey and acai puree in the blender.

Blend until thoroughly combined and smooth.

Pour the smoothie into 4 deep bowls.

Arrange the desired toppings over your smoothie bowls and serve.

TOP TIP PARENTS - blend a different choice of fruits for a change of recipe.

FUN FACT KIDS - Acai bowls originated in Brazil.

Nutritional value
Calories 187
Protein 5g
Carbs 43g
Fat 7g

Philly Eggs on Wholemeal Bagel

Parents and kids

3 wholemeal bagels
6 large eggs
1 heaped tsp butter
75g Philadelphia

Let's get cooking!

Break the eggs into a jug, add the butter and mix with a fork.

Heat a pan and pour in the eggs.

Cook over medium heat, occasionally stirring until almost set.

Meanwhile, toast the bagel and place onto warmed plates.

Spread the Philadelphia over the bagels and top with the egg.

Season with salt and black pepper.

TOP TIP PARENTS
- we love this with a slice of smoked salmon.

FUN FACT KIDS
- Eggs contain the highest quality protein you can buy.

Nutritional value
Calories 322
Protein 18g
Carbs 28g
Fat 14g

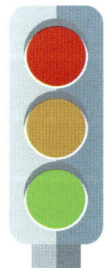

Parents

2 smoked bacon rashers
4 eggs
Handful closed cup
mushrooms
40g grated mozzarella
1 handful of spinach

Kids

1 slice of smoked bacon
2 eggs
Handful closed cup
mushrooms
25g grated mozzarella
1 handful spinach (Popeye!)

Breakfast Omelette

Let's get cooking!

Grown-ups, spritz the pan with fry light and heat it up.

Cut the bacon up into small pieces, and throw the bacon and mushrooms into the pan, cook them up and set aside.

Kids, help your grown-up crack the eggs into a bowl and whisk them up.

Grown-ups, back to you. Throw your pre-cooked bacon and mushrooms into the beaten egg mixture, along with the spinach, and add the omelette mixture to a heated pan.

When the omelette begins to cook and firm up, but there's still a little runny egg visible, sprinkle over the cheese. Using a spatula, ease around the edges of the omelette, and fold it in half.

When it starts to turn golden brown, the job is done. Slide the omelette onto a plate, and serve it up!

TOP TIP PARENTS
- Popeye helped increase American consumption of spinach by a third, let's hope we can do the same for your children.

TOP TIP KIDS
- Eating spinach will help give you muscles like Popeye (don't say we didn't try).

Nutritional value
Calories 280
Protein 22g
Carbs 2g
Fats 20g

Parents and kids

3 rashers of smoked bacon
2 Heck sausages
3 large eggs
300g of white potatoes
1 beef tomato
1 onion
A handful of button mushrooms
30g of grated Mozzarella cheese

The FF American Breakfast Mash Up

Let's get cooking!

Heat the oven to 200C/fan 180C and preheat your baking tray.

Peel and cut the potatoes into small chunks, roughly the same size as each other.

Tip them onto the hot baking tray, and roast for 1 hour or until golden and crispy. Turn the potatoes over once or twice during cooking.

Chop the bacon and sausages up into chunks.

Once the potatoes are cooked, heat a large pan and throw in the chopped bacon, mushrooms, onion, tomato, and chopped sausages. Sprinkle with garlic salt and pepper, and add the roasted potatoes.

Crack the eggs straight into the pan, and mash everything together. Top with mozzarella and leave to melt for 2 mins. Serve it all up and finish with a squirt of sauce.

TOP TIP PARENTS
- We recommend adding mustard to the pan at the end, it tastes great!

FUN FACT KIDS
- Jordan created this recipe, and it tastes way too good for a healthy option!

Nutritional value
Calories 305
Protein 22g
Carbs 28 g
Fats 14 g

The FF Big Weekend Vegan Breakfast

Parents
Sweet potato hash browns
8 asparagus spears
Handful of button mushrooms
Handful of spinach
½ tin of low salt baked beans
1 tomato, halved
1 avocado
2 chunks of sourdough
Vegan spread
Omega seeds

Kids
4 asparagus spears
Handful of button mushrooms
Handful of spinach
1/2 tin of reduced salt beans
1 tomato, halved
1 avocado
2 chunks of sourdough
Vegan spread
Omega seeds

Sweet potato hash browns
Half a large sweet potato, peeled and grated through the large grates of a box grater
4 Tbsp vegan spread
Salt
Pepper

TOP TIP PARENTS
- If you're thinking of going Vegan, one really useful place to start is by looking at some of your favourite recipes and thinking about how you might adapt them to be meatless and/or dairy-free. The big weekend Vegan breakfast is a great place to start.

FUN FACT KIDS
- Omega seeds- Just one tablespoon provides a good amount of protein, fibre and omega-3 fatty acids, in addition to being a rich source of some vitamins and minerals.

Let's get cooking!

Melt the vegan spread in a pan on a medium-high heat. Scoop large spoonsful of grated sweet potatoes into the pan forming small mounds. Gently press to spread the mounds out a bit. Sprinkle with salt and pepper. Cook undisturbed until they are nicely browned on one side, about 4 to 5 minutes, then carefully turn them over with a metal spatula to brown on the other side, 4 to 5 minutes more. When done, place on a baking tray in a warmed oven to keep warm until ready to eat.

Heat a pan over medium heat and throw in the asparagus, mushrooms, spinach and tomato halves. Sprinkle with salt and pepper and leave to cook.

Prepare the avocado into slices. Put the beans in a microwave safe bowl and heat for 2 mins, stir and heat again for another minute

Toast the sourdough whilst arranging everything from the pan on a plate, add your beans and avocado slices, then put the toasted sourdough to the side, and finish with a sprinkle of omega seeds.

Nutritional value
Calories350
Protein 11g
Carbs 41g
Fats 20g

Parents

4 slices of bacon unsmoked
4 eggs
Homemade beans
Portobello Mushrooms
Spinach
Tomatoes
2 slabs of sourdough

Kids

2 slices of bacon
2 eggs
Homemade beans
Portobello mushrooms
Spinach
Tomatoes
2 slabs of sourdough

Traditional Fry Up

Let's get cooking!

Heat the oil in a frying pan over medium heat. Add the tomato, bacon, mushrooms, and spinach.

When the tomato, bacon, mushrooms, and spinach are just about cooked, crack the eggs into the centre and allow to cook. You might want to add a little more oil just to crisp the edges.

Toast the slices of bread while the egg cooks, and heat your beans for 1 minute in the microwave. Serve everything on a plate, with the toast on the side.

TOP TIP PARENTS
- Heinz do a 'Five Beanz' snap pot, they take 1 min in the microwave. The beans include borlotti, cannellini, red kidney, pinto and haricot beans.

TOP TIP KIDS
- if five beanz are a little adventurous, we will let you swap for baked beans...just this once.

Nutritional value
Calories 440
Protein 36g
Carbs 39g
Fats 19g

3

LUNCHES

Parents and kids

240g wholewheat pasta
3 tins of tuna in spring water
1 red onion
1 tin of sweetcorn (198g)
Light mayo

Easy Tuna Pasta

Let's get cooking!

Peel and chop the red onion, then set aside.

Fill a large saucepan to three-quarters full with water and bring to the boil. Add the pasta and cook according to packet instructions until soft, then carefully drain using a colander.

Put the pasta back into the saucepan and add the red onion, tuna, sweetcorn, and mayonnaise, and mix everything together. Easy Peasy!

TOP TIP PARENTS AND KIDS
- double it up for later in the week, this makes a perfect lunchbox meal, and can be eaten hot or cold!

Nutritional value
Calories 319
Protein 29g
Carbs 18g
Fats 2g

Parents and kids
600g chicken breast
400g fresh penne pasta
12 cherry tomatoes
A generous bunch of spinach
3 tbsp of green pesto
1 tsp olive oil
1 jar of pesto sauce (or see the below ingredients to make your own)

To make your own pesto:
40g pine nuts
40g parmesan
70g basil (remove stalks)
120ml olive oil
1tsp garlic

Chicken Pesto Pasta

Let's get cooking!

Cook the pasta according to its package directions.

As the pasta cooks, heat the oil in a large pan over medium-high heat for 2 minutes.

Add the chicken and sprinkle over some salt, pepper, and garlic. Stir well to coat the chicken. Cook for 6-8 minutes, until the chicken, is cooked through, stirring occasionally. Remove the pan from the heat.

Add the cooked and drained pasta and the pesto to the pan with the chicken. Stir well.

To make your own pesto sauce
Gather the pesto ingredients and throw them all into a blender except the oil and cheese

Blend the ingredients to a paste

Stir in the oil and cheese, then add into the chicken pasta.

TOP TIP PARENTS AND KIDS
- this works well with a tomato-based sauce too, in case you fancy a change from pesto.

Nutritional value
Calories 319
Protein 29g
Carbs 18g
Fats 2g

Salmon and Rice

Parents
220g salmon
120g wholegrain rice
A handful of green beans
A handful of spinach
A bunch of tender stem broccoli
½ tsp chili
½ tsp garlic
Soy sauce

Kids
120g salmon
120g wholegrain rice
A handful of green beans
A handful of spinach
A bunch of tender stem broccoli

Let's get cooking!

Grown-ups! Heat a pan and fry the salmon skin side down for 6 minutes. Flip it over, and cook on the other side for 5 minutes.

Whilst the salmon is cooking, heat the rice in the microwave for two minutes.

Heat another pan, and add the green beans, spinach, and broccoli.

Add the rice to the pan with the salmon, and then throw in the cooked green beans, spinach, and broccoli.

Remove the little one's share and serve it up.

Give yours a kick by adding the garlic, chili and soy sauce to the pan. Leave it to cook for a further two minutes.

TOP TIP PARENTS
- buy your salmon frozen to save money.

FUN FACT KIDS
- Salmon is a great source of protein. Our body requires protein to heal, protect bone health, and prevent muscle loss, among other things.

Nutritional value
Calories 390
Protein 30g
Carbs 40g
Fats 14g

Sweet Potato Bowl

Bulk cook favourite

Parents and kids
600g sweet potatoes, diced
into small cubes
500g wholegrain rice
(2x micro-packets)
100g Pomegranate seeds
1 large head of broccoli, cut
into florets
Leafy salad
1 tsp of garlic
1 tbsp of olive oil
Vegan mayo

For the dressing:
2 tbsp almond butter
3 tbsp fresh orange juice,
to thin
2 tsp pure maple syrup
1/2 tsp apple cider vinegar
1 tsp of olive oil

Grown-ups! Preheat the oven to 200 C. Grease a baking tray with olive oil and set aside.

Place the diced sweet potatoes in a bowl, and microwave for 3-4 minutes to help pre-cook them.

Place broccoli florets, sweet potato cubes, and garlic on the baking tray. Drizzle olive oil over the top of the veggies, and toss to combine. Bake them for 20-30 minutes, or until the sweet potatoes are tender, stirring veggies & potatoes halfway through.

While the veggies roast: make the dressing by whisking together almond butter, orange juice, maple syrup, apple cider vinegar, and olive oil.

To assemble your meal prep tins, add 1/2 a bag of rice to each container, then top with roasted veggies, pomegranate seeds, and 1 1/2 tablespoons of the dressing. We like to add a splash of vegan mayo.

TOP TIP PARENTS AND KIDS- double up the ingredients and make a few days' worth, for a great on the go meal.

Nutrition value
Calories 445
Protein 13g
Carbs 60g
Fats 8g

Parents & Kids

1 egg
60ml milk
400 g white fish cut into
2cm thick chunks or strips
8 slices of wholegrain bread
65g plain flour
120g breadcrumbs

Fishfinger Sandwiches

Let's get cooking!

Preheat the oven to 200 degrees C.

Kids, help your grown up whisk the egg and milk together.

Coat the fish in flour, then dip the fish finger into the egg mixture, and roll it in breadcrumbs.

Grown-ups, lay the fish fingers on a lined baking tray, and spray with oil, bake for 15 minutes until golden brown and cooked through.

Lay the fishfingers on a surface of bread, then top with another slice to make your sandwich.

TOP TIP PARENTS
- This makes a great Fish shop Friday alternative.

FUN FACT KIDS
- Fish Finger inventor Clarence Birdseye launched them in 1955.

Nutritional value
Calories 490
Protein 30g
Carbs 58g
Fat 14g

Parents

4 slices of oven baked ham
4 slices of wholegrain bread
Lettuce leaves
Cucumber slices
Homemade Tomato chutney

Kids

2 slices of oven baked ham
2 slices of wholegrain bread
Lettuce
Cucumber slices
Homemade tomato chutney

The FF Classic Ham Sandwich

Tomato chutney

250 g red onions
500 g mixed-colour tomatoes
1 fresh red chili
75 ml red wine vinegar
140 g brown sugar

For the homemade chutney!

Peel and finely slice the onions, roughly chop the tomatoes, and deseed and finely slice the chili.

Put everything in a pan, season to taste and stir well to combine. Simmer for 30 to 40 minutes or until jammy. Pour into a jar and leave to cool. This will keep for up to 4 weeks in the fridge.

For the sandwich!

Spread your bread with the pre made chutney. Layer up your oven baked ham, lettuce leaves and cucumber slices.

Nutritional value

Calories 184
Protein 16g
Carbs 24g
Fats 1g

TOP TIP PARENTS
- the chutney is great on toast, and with a chunk of cheese. Also, there are 250 calories - so split between four this still make it a low calorie but delicious dressing. We fully recommend this!

FUN FACT KIDS
- Americans eat more than 300 million sandwiches every day.

Chickpea and Halloumi Salad

Parents and kids

2 tbsp olive oil
1 red onion, halved and sliced
200g cherry vine tomatoes
2 tsp harissa
250g Cooked lentils pouch
½ lemon, juiced
1 block of halloumi, cut into slices
1 tin of chickpeas (400g)
Small bunch of mint, roughly torn
Small bunch of parsley, roughly torn

Dressing

1 tbsp tahini
3 tbsp natural yogurt
2-3 tsp harissa
1 tsp runny honey
½ lemon, juiced
½ tsp garlic

Let's get prepping!

Heat a pan and cook the onion until soft. Stir in the tomatoes and cook until they are just starting to break down and burst open. Stir in the harissa, lentils and lemon juice, cook for a minute then season well and cool.

Whisk together all the dressing ingredients with enough water to make a drizzle-able consistency.

Fry the halloumi slices in batches in a dry non-stick pan until golden on both sides.

Toss the chickpeas and 1/2 the herbs into the lentil mixture.

Put on a platter or divide between plates and top with the dressing, the halloumi and the remaining herbs.

TOP TIP PARENTS
- this is a great take to work meal.

FUN FACT KIDS
- You might know of chickpeas as garbanzo beans. They are called chickpeas because of their unique shape that resembles the beak of a baby chick.

Nutritional value
Calories 327
Protein 14g
Carbs 25g
Fats 19g

The dressing: based on the whole dressing - 190 Calories

Parents and kids

180g smoked salmon
2 avocados
50g feta cheese
40g cashew nuts
6 walnuts chopped
Generous bunch of spinach
12 cherry tomatoes
2 tbsp olive oil

Carb Free Smoked Salmon

Let's get prepping!

Mix the feta, chopped walnuts and olive oil in a bowl.

Slice the avocado and tomatoes.

Arrange the spinach, avocado, and smoked salmon on a plate or prep container, then add the feta mix on top. Serve immediately and enjoy!

TOP TIP PARENTS
- this is a great on the go meal for work.

TOP TIP KIDS
- if smoked salmon is a little adventurous, swap it for cooked salmon instead.

Nutritional value
Calories 313
Protein 18g
Carbs 7g
Fats 28g

Parents and kids
500g of lean beef mince
4 whole meal wraps
1 tin of kidney beans, 240g
1 onion
2 mixed peppers
½ tsp garlic
1 tbsp ground cumin
1 tsp ground chili
1 tbsp dried coriander
1 tsp smoked paprika
1 tsp dried oregano
400 g tinned tomatoes

Guacamole
2 avocados - peeled, stones removed and chopped
½ tsp garlic
1 lime, juiced
salt and freshly ground black pepper to taste

Beef Burrito

Let's get cooking!

Heat some oil in a saucepan and gently fry the onion and garlic until cooked but still soft.

Add the mince beef, mixed peppers, and kidney beans. Continue to cook and stir, until the meat is browned.

Add the herbs, spices, and tomatoes. Stir thoroughly.

Simmer and occasionally stir for 15 minutes while you prepare the guacamole.

For the guacamole!

Destone the avocados and scoop the flesh onto a large board.

Add the juice from 1 lime, then season to taste with sea salt, black pepper and garlic.

Start chopping it all together until fine and well combined.

Heat the wraps in the microwave for 10 seconds, and serve it all up!

TOP TIP PARENTS
- this makes a great on the go meal.

TOP TIP KIDS
- take out the chili for smaller tastebuds.

Nutritional value
Calories 450
Protein 27g
Carbs 33g
Fats 17g

Hearty Veg Soup

Parents and kids

1 tbsp olive oil
1 large onion chopped
2 carrots chopped
2 celery sticks, chopped
50g dried red lentils
2 veg stock cubes
2 tbsp tomato purée
1 tbsp chopped fresh thyme
1 leek finely sliced
175g cauliflower
1 courgette chopped
1 ½ tsp garlic
½ large Savoy cabbage, stalks removed and leaves chopped
1 tbsp basil chopped

Let's get cooking!

Heat the oil in a large pan with a lid. Add the onion, carrots and celery and fry for 10 minutes, stirring from time to time until they are starting to brown around the edges. Stir in the lentils and cook for 1 minute more.

Follow the packet instructions to mix the vegetable stock cube, and add the liquid into the pan. Add in the tomato purée and thyme, and stir well. Add the leek, cauliflower, courgette, and garlic, then bring to the boil. Cover and leave to simmer for 15 minutes.

Add the cabbage and basil and cook for 5 minutes more until the veg is just tender. Season with pepper, ladle into bowls and serve.

TOP TIP PARENTS
- this will stay fresh in the fridge for up to 4 days, it can also be frozen.

TOP TIP KIDS
- Historical evidence of the existence of soup, dates all the way back to about 20,000 B.C!

Nutritional value
Calories 162
Protein7g
Carbs 19g
Fats 5g

Vegan Wrap

Let's get wrapping!

Parents and kids
2 avocados (stoned)
4 wholemeal vegan wraps
1 tbsp mustard
1 tbsp mango chutney
40g cashew nuts
Generous serving of fresh leaves

Kids, you can help with this one!

Get your grown-up to cut the avocado into slices.

In a bowl, mix the leaves, mustard, mango chutney and cashew nuts.

Distribute the mango chutney mix between the wraps, and layer with avocado.

TOP TIP PARENTS
- remove the mustard for littler taste buds.

FUN FACT KIDS
- avocado is a fruit, not a vegetable.

Nutritional value
Calories 238
Protein 5g
Carbs 33g
Fats 17g

Parents and kids

Vegan sausage (2 sausages
per person)
800g white potato cut into
quarters
400g parsnips
200g carrots
A few handfuls of tender
stem broccoli
1 tbsp maple syrup
2 vegan vegetable stock cubes
Corn flour to thicken gravy
4 homemade Yorkshire
puddings
½ tsp rosemary

Vegan Yorkshire pud

120g self-raising flour
½ tsp baking powder
200ml unsweetened soya
100ml water
4tsp veg oil

Vegan Sunday Lunch

Let's get cooking!

Preheat oven to 200C/180C fan, gas 6.

For the Yorkshire puddings, add all of the ingredients except the oil to a food processor with a pinch of salt and blitz until smooth. Transfer the batter to a jug, cover with cling film and leave to rest in the fridge for 1 hr.

Arrange the carrots and parsnips in a baking dish and spritz with fry light. Toss to evenly coat the vegetables. Pour the syrup over the coated vegetables, and season with salt and pepper. Bake in the preheated oven until vegetables are very tender, about 35 minutes.

Spoon a tsp of oil into eight holes of a muffin tin and place in the oven for 5 mins to get really hot. Remove the tin from the oven and carefully pour the batter into the hot oil. Return to the oven and bake for 25-30 mins until risen and deep golden brown.

TOP TIP PARENTS
- Tofurky Italian Sausages are our favourite.

FUN FACT KIDS
- Vegans save 1,100 gallons of water each day.

Nutritional value
Calories 515 g
Protein 19g
Carbs 60g
Fats 10g

Place potatoes in a large roasting pan and toss with oil, salt, pepper, and rosemary until evenly coated. Spread out potatoes in a single layer. Bake in the oven for 20 minutes, stirring occasionally.

Preheat Hob and pan on a medium setting, spritz with fry light. Place the sausages and broccoli into the pan. Cook on a medium heat for 8 minutes, turning frequently. Check the food is piping hot.

Mix 2 vegan vegetable stock cubes with 500ml of boiling water, stir and Siv in the corn flour to thicken as desired

Plate everything up, let it swim in gravy, and enjoy!

Parents and kids
Beef joint (1 kg)
800g white potato
400g parsnips
200g carrots
A few handfuls of tender
stem broccoli
2 beef stock cubes
Corn flour to thicken gravy
4 homemade Yorkshire
puddings

Homemade Yorkshire puddings
2 large eggs
200g self-raising flower
200ml semi skimmed milk

Sunday Lunch

Let's get cooking!

Preheat the oven to gas 3, 170°C, fan 150°C.

For the Yorkshire puddings, add all of the ingredients except the oil to a food processor with a pinch of salt and blitz until smooth. Transfer the batter to a jug, cover with cling film and leave to rest in the fridge for 1 hr.

Put the beef in a large ovenproof casserole dish with a lid, and surround with the potatoes and vegetables. Cover with the lid, and cook in the oven for 1 1/2 hours, undisturbed. Set aside to stand for 10 minutes.

Spoon a tsp of oil into eight holes of a muffin tin and place in the oven for 5 mins to get really hot. Remove the tin from the oven and carefully pour the batter into the hot oil. Return to the oven and bake for 25-30 mins until risen and deep golden brown.

Remove the beef and vegetables from the casserole, using a slotted spoon and transfer to a warm serving dish, loosely cover with foil to keep warm and don't discard the meat juices.

Nutritional value
Calories 556
Protein 40g
Carbs 55g
Fats 20g

Pour the juices from the beef into a jug, add in the stock cubes and sieve in corn flour carefully to thicken as desired.

Slice the beef and serve with the vegetables, Yorkshire puddings and gravy.

4

DINNERS

Parents and kids

600g chicken
500g Microwave wild rice (2 packets)
1 bake in the bag (we like Maggi garlic chicken)
4 small corn on the cobs

Bake in the Bag Chicken with Wild Rice

Let's get cooking!

Preheat over to 180C/160C fan, gas 4. Do not exceed this temperature. Remove and unfold the cooking bag from top of the sachet, keeping the red tie for later use. Place the chicken into the bag. Add the seasoning from sachet into the bag.

Close the bag at the end using the red tie. Mix together by gently massaging the seasoning into the ingredients. Place the bag on its side into a large ovenproof dish, spreading out the ingredients. Do not pierce the bag. Place dish on the bottom shelf of the oven. The bag expands so ensure there is enough space between racks.

Cook for 35-40 minutes. Remove from the oven, leave to stand for 2-3 minutes before opening - the steam will be very hot. Ensure that the chicken is fully cooked through and piping hot.

TOP TIP PARENTS

- Try different flavour bake in the bags, switch up the chicken, we like to bake thighs, wings, legs and breast.

FUN FACT KIDS

-Wild rice is a special type of grain that's chewy and tasty. It's higher in protein than regular rice, and it contains several important nutrients and an impressive amount of antioxidants.

Nutritional value

Calories 400g
Protein 36g
Carbs 45g
Fats 7g

Put the cobs of corn on a microwave safe plate and microwave on high for 5 mins. Throw the wild rice in the microwave for 2 mins, then repeat with the second bag. Serve it all up!

Parents and kids

3 large sweet potatoes
3 tins of tuna in spring water
1 red onion
1 tin of sweetcorn (198g)
Light mayo (we like vegan mayo)
2 tbsp olive oil

Sweet Jacket Potato with Tuna Mayo

Let's get baking!

Preheat over to 180C/160C fan, gas 4.

Rinse the sweet potatoes, pat dry, and rub with a little olive oil. Roast on a baking tray for about 40 minutes, (or prick with a fork and cook in the microwave for 10 to 12 minutes).

Peel and finely dice the red onion, drain the sweetcorn and tuna.

Add the chopped red onion, drained sweetcorn and tuna, and light mayo in a bowl.

Mix together and leave the tuna mix to the side.

Once the sweet potatoes are cooked, halve one for the children, slice into yours and then top them all with the tuna mix.

TOP TIP PARENTS AND KIDS

- pre-baked sweet potatoes stay fresh in the fridge for around 5 days, they can also be frozen making it a quick, cost effective lunch option.

Nutritional value

Calories 300 g
Protein 28g
Carbs 45g
Fats 3g

Bang Bang Vegan Stir-Fry

Parents & Kids

400g Udon noodles
4 tbsp corn flour
Pinch of salt
300g tofu, diced
2 tbsp olive oil
2 tsp easy ginger
1 tsp chili
½ tin of sweetcorn (80g)
1 carrot chopped finely
100g mangetout
Small handful of coriander
½ lime wedges to garnish
Peanut sauce
2 tbsp peanut butter organic
2 tbsp soy sauce
1 tbsp olive oil
½ lime (juiced)

Let's get cooking!

Bring a saucepan of water to boil, add in your noodles and cook to the packet instructions, cool with cold running water and drain well.

Whisk together the peanut sauce ingredients, and add a dash of hot water if it's a little thick.

Mix the corn flour and salt together in a bowl, throw in the tofu, mix it around to coat it, then remove and shake away the excess flour.

Heat the oil in a wok or frying pan over medium heat, add the coated tofu and fry for 4 mins. Carefully remove the tofu and set aside, then return the empty pan to the heat. Add the sweetcorn, chili, garlic, ginger, carrot, mangetout and courgette. Stir-fry for 3 mins. Take the pan off the heat.

Add the tofu, noodles, peanut sauce and coriander to the pan, and toss everything together to warm through. Finish with a squeeze of lime and divide between plates.

TOP TIP PARENTS
- Add vegan vegetable stock cubes to turn the recipe into a broth.

FUN FACT KIDS
- Udon noodles are long, thick white noodles that traditionally hail from Osaka and southern Japanese regions.

Nutritional value
Calories 430
Protein 23g
Carbs 34g
Fats 22g

Parents & Kids

10 heck sausages
800g white potatoes
40g unsalted butter
Gravy granules
1 onion

Bangers and Mash

Let's get cooking!

Peel and cook the potatoes in boiling salted water for 10-12 minutes or until soft.

Spritz a pan with fry light, and heat over a medium heat, add the onion and sausages, and cook for 6-8 mins.

Drain the potatoes and mash in the butter.

Pile the mash onto four warmed serving plates. Divide the sausage and onions on the mounds of mash. Mix the granules according to packet instructions, and finally drizzle over the gravy.

TOP TIP PARENTS
- Heck sausages come in all different flavours, they also do a vegan range.

FUN FACT KIDS
- The term "bangers" came from sausages made during World War I, when there were meat shortages, sausages were made with such a high-water content, that they were more liable to pop under high heat when cooked.

Nutritional value
Calories 335
Protein 27.5g
Carbs 33g
Fat 10g

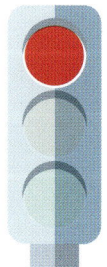

Parents & Kids

6 boneless chicken thighs
1 tin chopped tomatoes
(400g)
1 tbsp tomato puree
1 tsp cumin
2 tsp garam masala
1 tsp chili powder
3 tsp garlic
2 packets microwave rice

Mild Chicken Curry

Let's get cooking!

Spritz a pan with fry light and heat over a medium heat, cut the thighs into chunks and throw them in the pan.

Leave to cook for 12 mins and then add the onion and spices, cook until the onions have browned.

Add the tinned tomatoes and tomato puree, and let the chicken mix simmer for a further 10 mins.

Microwave the rice, split between plates, and top with the curry.

TOP TIP PARENTS
- Switch the chicken to Tofu to create a vegetarian curry.

FUN FACT KIDS
- The first curry recipe was published in a British cookbook in 1747.

Nutritional value
Calories 451
Protein 45g
Carbs 32g
Fat 14g

Chickpea Curry

Parents and kids

For the paste
2 tbsp oil
1 onion, diced
1 tsp chili
1 small bulb of garlic
(9 cloves)
Thumb-sized piece ginger,
peeled
1 tbsp ground coriander
2 tbsp ground cumin
1 tbsp garam masala
2 tbsp tomato purée

For the curry

2 x 400g cans chickpeas,
drained
400g can chopped tomatoes
100g creamed coconut
½ small pack coriander,
chopped, plus extra to garnish
100g spinach

To serve

2 packets of microwave rice

TOP TIP PARENTS
- Add a few poppadoms for
a weekend treat.

FUN FACT KIDS
- A record tower of 1,280
poppadoms was piled up in
Northampton to celebrate
Curry Week in 2012. It was
5ft 8in high.

Let's get cooking!

Heat a little oil in a frying pan, add the diced onion and chili, and cook for 8 mins.

In a food processor, combine 9 garlic cloves, a thumb-sized piece of peeled ginger, and the remaining oil, then add the ground coriander, ground cumin, garam masala, tomato purée, and the fried onion. Blend to a smooth paste – add a drop of water or more oil, if needed.

Cook the paste in a saucepan for 2 mins over a medium heat, stirring occasionally so it doesn't stick.

Tip in the drained chickpeas, and the chopped tomatoes, and simmer for 5 mins until reduced down.

Add 100g creamed coconut with a little water, cook for 5 mins more, then add the chopped coriander, and 100g spinach, cook until wilted.

Garnish with extra coriander, microwave the rice for 2 mins, and serve it all up.

Nutritional value
Calories 514
Protein 11g
Carbs 52g
Fats 28g

Parents & Kids

1 onion, sliced
1 red pepper, thickly sliced
small bunch fresh coriander, stalks finely chopped
1 tbsp olive oil
500g low fat beef mince
salt and freshly ground black pepper
2 fat garlic cloves, crushed
1 tsp ground cumin
1 tsp ground coriander
2 tsp hot chilli powder
1 tsp dried oregano
2 tbsp tomato purée
1 can chopped tomatoes (400g)
300ml hot beef stock
2 x cans of red kidney beans in water, rinsed and drained
1 cube good quality dark chocolate, minimum 70% cocoa solids

TOP TIP PARENTS
- If you're short on time in the morning, prepare everything you need for your slow-cooked meal the night before, put it into the slow-cooker dish, cover and store in the fridge overnight.

FUN FACT KIDS- 'Chilli Con Carne' originated from Texas.

Sophie's Slow Cooker Chilli

Let's get slow cooking!

Place the onion, red pepper and coriander stalks into a slow cooker. Heat the oil in a large non-stick frying pan, season the beef with salt and freshly ground black pepper, then fry in two batches until golden-brown, transferring to the slow cooker when ready.

Add the garlic, spices and oregano to the pan juices, and fry for one minute until fragrant. Stir in the tomato purée, tomatoes and stock then bring to a boil. Pour the hot sauce over the meat, then cover with a lid and cook on low for seven hours. Stir in the beans, then cook for an hour more until the meat is very tender.

Pop the chocolate into the sauce, let it melt, then stir it in. Season the sauce to your taste, then scatter with the coriander leaves and serve.

Nutritional value
Calories 330
Protein 32g
Carbs 15g
Fat 10g

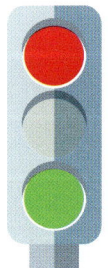

Parents & Kids

600g white potato
2 tsp olive oil
300g breadcrumbs
3 white fish fillets, such as haddock
2tbsp plain flour
2 eggs
1 tin mushy peas

Fish and Chips

Let's get cooking!

Heat the oven to 200C/180C fan, gas 6.

Peel and chop the potatoes into thick chips, then toss with the olive oil and some salt. Arrange on a large non-stick baking tray, and roast for 20 mins, turning halfway.

Dust the fish in flour, shaking off the excess, then crack and beat the eggs. Dip the fish into the egg, then the breadcrumbs to coat thoroughly. Roast the fish with the chips for a further 20 mins, until both are golden.

Just before the fish and chips are ready, microwave the peas according to the instructions.

Serve it all up.

TOP TIP PARENTS
- Popular kinds of white fish are tilapia, cod, bass, grouper, haddock, catfish, and snapper, if you fancy trying something new.

FUN FACT KIDS
- The longest running fish and chip shop still in operation is based in Yeadon, near Leeds.

Nutritional value
Calories 484
Carbs 58g
Protein 42g
Fat 11g

Parents & Kids
2 tbsp olive oil
1kg chicken thighs and drumsticks
1 bottle jerk barbecue sauce
1 bunch spring onions, sliced

For the rice and peas
2x microwave basmati rice
2 x cans kidney beans
400g can coconut milk
1 bunch spring onions, chopped
1 thyme sprig
1 tsp garlic
1 tsp allspice

Jerk Chicken

Let's get cooking!

Heat the oven to 220C/200C fan, gas 7.

Heat the oil in a roasting tin, then carefully add the chicken. Brown them lightly on all sides – it will take about 6-8 mins. Pour over the jerk sauce, scatter over the sliced spring onions, then toss to coat each piece of chicken.

Roast the chicken for 30 mins, turning occasionally.

While the chicken is cooking, make the rice & peas.

Bring a pan of water to the boil with the liquid only from the kidney beans, the coconut milk, spring onions, thyme, garlic, allspice and some salt, then simmer for 2 mins. Add the microwaved rice and beans, then simmer for 5 mins more.

Drain and serve straight away with the chicken.

TOP TIP PARENTS
- Switch Jerk BBQ sauce, to regular BBQ for less spice.

FUN FACT KIDS
- Jerk is a style of cooking native to Jamaica.

Nutritional value
Calories 937
Carbs 86g
Protein 46g
Fat 48g

Parents & Kids

6 tbsp crunchy organic peanut butter
3 tbsp satay sauce
3 tbsp dark soy sauce
1 tbsp brown sugar
3 tsp garlic
Pinch of salt
300ml water
1 tbsp groundnut oil
1 onion, chopped
1 green pepper, thinly sliced
20 uncooked king prawns
1 tbsp corn flour (mixed with 2 tbsp water)
½ lime juiced
2 bags of micro rice

King Prawn Satay

Let's get cooking!

Put the peanut butter, satay sauce, soy sauce, sugar, garlic, ½ tsp of salt and water in a medium saucepan and mix well to combine.

Bring to the boil, then remove from the heat and set aside.

Heat the oil in a wok or pan over medium heat, add the onion and pepper, and stir fry for 2 mins.

Throw in the prawns and the remaining salt, and stir-fry for 1 min. Pour in the sauce and re heat until hot. If the sauce is too thin, carefully pour in the corn flour mix little by little until it has thickened up.

Microwave the rice, divide between plates and top with the king prawn satay.

Nutritional value
Calories 404
Protein 17g
Carbs 36g
Fat 21g

TOP TIP
PARENTS
- How to peel and de-vein the prawns.

Step 1:
To peel prawns, remove the head and legs. Peel the shells from the prawns. Squeeze the tail to remove it from the body, if desired.

Step 2:
To devein a prawn, use a small sharp knife to make a slit along the middle of the back to expose the dark vein. Pull out the vein.

Step 3:
To devein a prawn without cutting the back, use your fingers to carefully pull the vein through the opening at the head end to remove.

FUN FACT KIDS
- Shrimp are low in calories, high in protein.

Lentil Cottage Pie

Parents and kids

1kg of white potatoes peeled and chopped
1 tbsp olive oil
1 red onion
1 courgette
4 carrots
3 red peppers
2 fresh tomatoes
500ml veg stock
1 can chopped tomatoes (400g)
200g green lentils
1 tsp smoked paprika
2 bay leaves
3 tbsp dairy free spread
6 tbsp unsweetened almond milk

Pre-heat the oven to 200C/180C fan.

Add the potatoes to a large pan of boiling water, and boil for 20 mins until tender.

Peel and chop all the veg into chunks. Heat a pan over medium heat, and throw in all the veg except the tomatoes. Season well and leave to cook for 5 mins. Add the tomatoes and leave the mix to cook for another 10 mins.

Add the stock, canned tomatoes, tomato puree and 150ml of water into the saucepan. Stir in the lentils and simmer for 20 mins, throw in the paprika and bay leaves then give it a good stir.

Drain the potatoes and return them to the pan, mash in the dairy free spread and milk.

Transfer the lentil mix to an ovenproof dish, spoon over the potato and sprinkle with paprika. Bake in the oven for 20 mins and divide between bowls once cooked.

TOP TIP PARENTS
- If you're not big on lentils, replace them for chickpeas.

FUN FACT KIDS
- Lentils have been found in Egyptian tombs dating as far back as 2400 BC.

Nutritional value
Calories 324
Protein 10g
Carbs 61g
Fat 5g

Parents & Kids

For the burgers
1 tbsp olive oil
1 red onion, finely chopped
500g lean minced beef
1 egg
12 cream crackers, bashed to fine crumbs
2 tsp chili
2 tsp garlic
1 tsp each, tomato ketchup and brown sauce
2 tbsp plain flour

For the wedges

4 sweet potatoes, cut into wedges
2 tbsp olive oil
1 tsp paprika

Burger relish

4 large tomatoes
1 red onion, finely chopped
1 tsp garlic
2 tbsp olive oil
1/2 tsp chili
Salt and pepper
1 tbsp tomato puree
2 tsp dark soy sauce

Naked Burger

Let's get cooking!

Heat the oil in a frying pan, and fry the onion for about 5 mins or until soft. Leave to cool slightly, then put the onion in a large bowl with the mince, egg, bashed crackers, chili, garlic, ketchup and brown sauce, and mix well to combine. Divide the mince into 6 balls, and flatten each into a nice fat burger.

Put the flour on a plate, dab each burger to the flour on both sides, then transfer to a baking tray. Wrap with cling film and pop in the fridge for a couple of hours.

Heat oven to 200C/180C fan.

To make the wedges, put the sweet potato on a baking tray and spritz with fry light. Sprinkle with paprika, season, then give them a good shake or shuffle around with your hands to make sure they're well coated. Roast for 30 mins. Make sure you give them a good shake a couple of times to ensure they cook evenly.

FUN FACT KIDS
- Nearly 60-percent of all sandwiches sold worldwide are actually hamburgers.

Nutritional value
Calories 610
Protein 35g
Carbs 70g
Fat 21g

When the wedges have been cooking for 10 mins, drizzle the burgers with a little olive oil and put them in the oven to cook with the wedges for the remaining 20-30 mins, flipping them halfway.

For the relish, place all of the ingredients in a pan with salt and pepper. When it starts to bubble, simmer for about 15 minutes, until the tomatoes have cooled down.

Serve the burgers, top with relish and finish with sweet potato wedges.

TOP TIP
PARENTS

- Prepare the burger mixture, form into patties, and place them in a single layer in a freezer bag and freeze immediately. They can be kept in this frozen state for up to 3 months.

Parents & Kids

250g wholemeal flour, plus a little for kneading
1 tsp instant yeast
¼ tsp salt
1 tbsp rapeseed oil
For the topping
pack of 3 peppers, sliced
1 large onion, sliced
1 tbsp rapeseed oil
1 tsp fennel seeds
2 tbsp barbecue sauce
2 tbsp tomato purée
1 large skinless chicken breast fillet (about 225g), diced
175g baby plum tomatoes, quartered
50g Applewood smoked cheese, grated

Homemade Pizza

Let's get cooking!

Heat the oven to 220C/200C fan, gas 7.

Tip the flour into a bowl and add the yeast, salt, oil and warm water, then mix well to a very soft dough. Tip the dough onto a work surface, and knead for about 10 mins. The dough is sticky, but try not to add too much extra flour. Leave in the bowl and cover with a tea towel.

Toss the peppers and onions with the oil and fennel seeds, then roast for 15 mins. Meanwhile mix the barbecue sauce and tomato purée with 5 tbsp water.

Take the dough and press into pizza bases. Spread with two thirds of the barbecue sauce mix, then add the remainder to the chicken and toss well to coat it.

Take the roasted pepper mixture from the oven, and spread on top of the pizza. Scatter over the tomatoes, then evenly spoon on the barbecue chicken. Scatter with the cheese and bake for 15 mins.

TOP TIP PARENTS
- You can freeze the pizza dough in well-wrapped 1/2-lb balls for up to 3 weeks.

FUN FACT KIDS
-The United States eats 350 slices of pizza every second.

Nutritional value
Calories 448
Protein 14g
Carbs 54g
Fats 11g

Parents and kids
500g turkey mince
1 tin chopped tomatoes
(400g)
1 tin of kidney beans
6 slabs of sourdough
100g grated mozzarella
1 tbsp olive oil
1 large onion, chopped
2 celery sticks finely chopped
1 red pepper
1 tsp chili
2 tsp smoked paprika
1 tsp ground cumin
1 tbsp tomato puree
200 ml chicken stock

Sloppy Joes

Let's get cooking!

Heat the oil in a large pan over medium heat. Throw In the onion, carrots, and celery, and cook for 8 mins. Add the red pepper and garlic, and cook for 5 mins more. Stir in the chili, paprika, cumin and add the mince. Cook for 5 mins, and stir in the mince making sure it has evenly browned.

Add the tomatoes, tomato puree, stock, and season well. Simmer over a low heat for 1 hour.

15 mins before the end of cooking, throw in the beans.

Preheat the grill to medium.

Lay the sourdough over the mince mixture, and scatter the cheese. Put the whole saucepan under the hot grill for 2-3 mins, until the cheese is melted, and serve it straight up.

TOP TIP PARENTS
- We like to use lean beef mince for this recipe too.

FUN FACT KIDS
- Sloppy joes are often called by different names in different parts of the United States, such as barbecues, dynamites, goulash, sloppy janes, slushburgers, steamers, wimpies and yum yums.

Nutritional value
Calories 429
Protein 42g
Carbs 34g
Fat 12g

The FF Soy and Butter Pasta

Parents and kids
350g spaghetti
1tbsp olive oil
3 tsp garlic
200g shiitake mushrooms, sliced
3 tbsp soy sauce
40g unsalted butter
(swap for vegan spread)
A small handful of chopped chives
Sea salt and black pepper

Let's get cooking!

Cook the pasta in a large saucepan of boiling water for 8-10 mins until just cooked. Drain the pasta but set aside one cup of the cooking water.

Heat the oil in a frying pan and fry the garlic and mushrooms until browned, we recommend 5-6 mins.

Add the soy sauce and butter to the mushrooms, allow them to bubble and then add the cooked pasta along with a tbsp of the cooking water and mix well. Add the chives and season to taste before serving.

ALTERNATIVE - If you fancy swapping spaghetti for zucchini, here's a quick recipe that explains how:

Slice the zucchini into thinner strips resembling spaghetti. Heat olive oil in a frying pan over medium heat then cook and stir zucchini in the hot oil for 1 minute. Add water and cook until zucchini is softened - 5 to 7 minutes. Season with salt and pepper.

Nutritional value
Calories 250
Protein 6g
Carbs 27g
Fat 12g

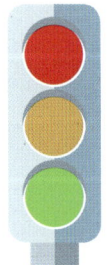

FUN FACT KIDS - January 4th is National Spaghetti Day.

Parents & kids

1 tbsp olive oil
200g lean steak mince
1 onion, finely chopped
4 large mushrooms, sliced
1 carrot, grated
1 tin of chopped tomatoes
1 vegetable stock cube, mixed
with 230ml hot water
2 tbsp tomato purée
½ tsp Worcestershire sauce
1 tsp black pepper
300g wholewheat spaghetti
2 tbsp chopped fresh parsley

Spag Boll

Let's get cooking!

Heat the oil in a large saucepan over a medium heat. Add the mince and the onion, and fry for five mins, occasionally stirring, until the mince is browned and the onions have softened.

Add the mushrooms and carrot, cook for around one min, then add tinned tomatoes, vegetable stock, tomato purée, Worcestershire sauce and black pepper. Stir well and bring to the boil, then reduce the heat to simmer for 15-20 minutes, until the sauce has thickened.

Place the wholemeal spaghetti in a deep saucepan full of salted boiling water, and cook according to packet instructions, then drain.

To serve, divide the cooked spaghetti between four dishes, top with portions of Bolognese sauce, and sprinkle with parsley.

TOP TIP PARENTS
- remove the kid's portion of sauce, and add a splash (or few) of red wine to yours.

FUN FACT KIDS
- The earliest documented recipe for a meat-based sauce served with pasta, comes from the late 18th century Imola, near Bologna.

Nutritional value
Calories 270
Protein 17g
Carbs 29g
Fat 7g

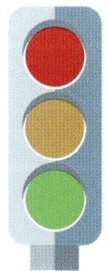

Parents and kids

3 fillet steaks
3 baked potato's
2 tsp olive oil
A few handfuls of button mushrooms
A few handfuls of asparagus spears

The FF steak sauce

1 egg yolk
30g double cream
1 tsp soy sauce
1 tsp English mustard
1 tbsp olive oil
Salt and pepper

Fillet Steak with FF Homemade Sauce

Let's get cooking!

Preheat the oven to 200C/180C fan, gas 6. Wash and dry the potatoes, then pierce each potato 2-3 times with a fork. Rub oil, salt and pepper over the potatoes. place them on a baking sheet, and bake for about 45 minutes. The exact baking time will depend on how large the potatoes are. Poke a fork into the centre of the baked potato to check its soft.

For the sauce, add all of the sauce ingredients into a jug and whisk together. Set aside until later.

Heat two pan's over medium heat and spritz with fry light. Throw the asparagus in one pan, and leave to cook for 5 mins. Add the mushrooms in with the asparagus and cook for a further 5 mins.

TOP TIP PARENTS
- We like sirloin steak, it's boneless, lean and a good value for this fairly tender cut.

FUN FACT KIDS
- Red meat provides protein, which helps build bones and muscles.

Nutritional value
Calories 420
Protein 34g
Carbs 27g
Fat 18g

The sauce
Calories 324 for the whole thing
80cals per serving

While the veg is cooking, add the steaks to the other pan. Cook the steak for 2-3 minutes each side for rare, 4 minutes each side for medium, and 5-6 minutes each side for well-done. Transfer the steak to plates, and set aside for 3-5 minutes to rest. Add the sauce into the steak pan, and allow to heat up for 2 mins. Add the jacket potato's, veg and sauce to the steak plates.

Parents & Kids

350 g lean beef steak cut into chunks
1 tbsp olive oil
1 large red onion, peeled and finely diced
1 large carrot, peeled and finely diced
1 celery stick, finely diced
1 red pepper, chopped
1 tsp Garlic
2 sprigs fresh thyme, leaves only
2 large mushrooms, diced
Salt and pepper
1 tbsp plain whole meal flour
1 tbsp tomato puree
1 tbsp Worcestershire Sauce
500ml beef stock
1 sheet puff pastry
1 tbsp milk for brushing pastry

The FF Steak Pie

Let's get cooking!

Preheat your oven to 150C.

Heat the olive oil in a large frying pan over medium heat and brown the beef until golden, set aside.
In the same pan, cook the onion, carrot, celery and garlic for 4-5 minutes. Add in the thyme and mushrooms, and cook for a further 2 minutes. Season to taste, then add the flour and tomato paste, stirring well for 1 minute.

Place the beef back into the pan and add the stock and Worcestershire sauce. Bring to the boil, then reduce the heat to low and cover. Bake in the oven for 90 mins.

Remove the pastry sheet from the freezer and allow to thaw whilst the pie mix is baking. Increase the heat of the oven to 190C. Place the beef filling into an ovenproof dish and cover with the pastry, tucking into the sides. Brush the top with milk and bake in the oven for around 25 minutes or until golden brown on top.

TOP TIP PARENTS
- Freshly baked steak pie will keep for about 3 to 5 days in the fridge; refrigerate covered with foil or plastic wrap.

FUN FACT KIDS
- Ancient Greeks are believed to have originated pie pastry.

Nutritional value
Calories 610
Protein 38g
Carbs 30g
Fats 35g

Sweet Potato Cottage Pie

Parents & Kids

1kg sweet potato, peeled and cut into chunks
500g lean beef mince
1 onion, chopped
120g frozen peas
200g chopped carrots
1 tsp garlic
25g unsalted butter
200ml passata
Gravy granules

Let's get cooking!

Bring a saucepan of water to boil and throw in the sweet potatoes, boil for 15 mins until tender, drain well, then mash with butter, season to taste and set aside.

Heat a large pan over medium heat, and spritz with fry light. Throw in the onion, and fry for 2 mins, then add the garlic, peas, and carrot, cook until soft.

Meanwhile, heat the remaining oil in a separate frying pan, and fry the mince in batches, scooping each batch out with a slotted spoon to leave any excess oil behind.

Add the mince to the veg, stir in the passata, and bring to a simmer.

Layer the mince mix in an oven proof dish, top with the sweet potato mash, and heat the oven to 190/170C fan, gas 5. Cook for 20 mins if cooking straightaway, or for 40 mins from chilled, until golden and hot all the way through.

Nutritional value
Calories 450
Protein 29g
Carbs 57g
Fats 8g

TOP TIP PARENTS-
The pie can be covered and chilled for 2 days, or frozen for up to a month.

FUN FACT KIDS-
Sweet potatoes offer other nutrients such as potassium, iron and vitamin B-6.

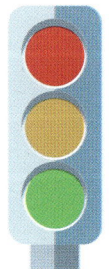

Parents & kids

For the dough
200ml water
1tsp active dried yeast
250g of strong white bread flour
Plus, extra for dusting
Pich of sea salt
2tbsp olive oil

For the puree

1 tbsp olive oil
1 onion, chopped
2 tsp garlic
1 can chopped tomatoes (400g)
1 tbsp tomato puree
Handful of fresh oregano
Pinch of sea salt and black pepper
Choice of toppings e.g. cherry tomatoes, spinach, black olives, broccoli, artichokes, vegan mozzarella, red bell peppers, mushrooms.

FUN FACT PARENTS
- Pizza dough will last approximately three days in the fridge.

TOP TIP KIDS
- The number of vegans in Britain has doubled twice in the past four years.

Vegan Pizza

Let's get pizza making!

Kids, mix together the water (lukewarm), and yeast in a jug. Set aside for 5 mins to let the yeast activate.

Mix together the flour and salt in a large mixing bowl. Add the yeast mixture to the flour and pour in the oil. The mixture will feel quite wet, so stir it with your hands until it comes together.

Sprinkle some flour onto a work surface and knead the dough, add additional flour if you need to. Once the dough is smooth, portion into 6 balls. Place the dough balls onto a lightly oiled baking tray, and cover the tray with a damp tea towel, leave them to rise for an hour.

For the sauce
Grown up's, heat the oil in a pan over medium heat. Throw in the onion, garlic, tomatoes, oregano and tomato puree. Stir well and let it simmer for 5 mins. Blitz the sauce in a food processor for a few seconds.

Heat the oven to 200C/180C fan, gas 6. Kids, roll the dough balls into pizzas, smother on the sauce, and sprinkle with toppings. Pass to your grown-up to bake in the oven for 12 mins, until the edges are golden.

Nutritional value
Calories 648
Protein 16g
Carbs 88g
Fats 17g

Veggie Fajitas

Parents & Kids
1 tin black beans, drained (400g)
small bunch coriander, finely chopped
8-12 small flour tortillas
1 avocado, sliced
2 tbsp soured cream

For the fajita mix
1 red and 1 yellow pepper, cut into strips
1 tbsp oil
1 red onion, cut into thin wedges
1 tsp garlic
½ tsp chili powder
½ tsp smoked paprika
½ tsp ground cumin
1 lime, juiced

Let's get cooking!

Heat the oil in a frying pan over medium heat, add the pepper and onion, and fry until soft.

Add the garlic and cook for 1 min, then add the spices and stir. Cook for a couple of mins more until the spices become aromatic, then add half the lime juice and season.

Transfer to a dish, leaving any juices behind, and keep them warm. Tip the black beans into the same pan, then add the remaining lime juice and plenty of seasoning. Stir the beans around the pan to warm them through and help them absorb any flavors of the fajita mix, then stir through the coriander.

Warm the tortillas in a microwave , then wrap them so they don't dry out. Serve the tortillas with the fajita mix, beans, avocado and soured cream for everyone to help themselves.

TOP TIP PARENTS
- If veggie fajitas aren't your thing, add in 500g of chicken to the recipe.

FUN FACT KIDS
- The fajita is truly a Tex-Mex food (a blending of Texas cowboy and Mexican foods).

Nutrtional value
Calories 463
Protein 12g
Carbs 55g
Fats 19g

Parents & Kids

1 tbsp olive oil
1 onion, finely chopped
2 tsp garlic
1 tsp smoked paprika
½ tsp ground cumin
1 tbsp dried thyme
3 carrots, sliced
2 medium sticks celery,
finely sliced
1 red pepper, chopped
1 yellow pepper, chopped
2 x 400g cans tomatoes
1 vegetable stock cube, made
up to 250ml
2 courgettes, sliced thickly
2 sprigs fresh thyme
250g cooked lentils

Veggie Casserole

Let's get cooking!

Heat the oil in a large pan, add the onion and cook for 8 mins until softened. Add the garlic, paprika, ground cumin, thyme, carrots, celery, and peppers. Cook for 5 minutes.

Add both tins of tomatoes, vegetable stock, courgettes, and 2 sprigs of thyme. Cook for 20 - 25 minutes.

Take out the thyme sprigs then stir the lentils, and bring back to a simmer.

Divide between bowls and enjoy!

Nutritional value
Calories 216
Protein 12.3g
Carbs 31g
Fats 5.1g

Afterthoughts ...

How to TRY and sleep well
(we know, it's easier said than done).

1. Keep caffeine and alcohol to a minimum (yes, even if the kids have been hard work!).
2. Consistency is key; a set bedtime routine will help yourself and the little ones get into a good sleeping pattern.
3. Exercise is great, but try and give yourself time to wind down before settling into bed.
4. Don't go to bed on an empty stomach, hunger pains can keep you restless, a full tum is great for the best chance of a good night's sleep.

Stay Hydrated

Staying hydrated is one of the most important things you can do. Sometimes remembering to drink enough water can be difficult so here are some ways to make it easier …

1. Add fruit to your bottle; we like to use lemon and mint.
2. Try to drink a full glass of water with every meal.
3. Try to incorporate water intake into your daily routine by breaking up times in the day. Aim to have drunk a certain amount by each time you have chosen. For example, three litres of water a day would mean consuming your first litre by midday, your second by four pm and finally your last litre by the time you go to bed.
4. Buy a bottle to use that you can keep refilling with water and carry it with you at all times. One of the main reasons that many of us don't drink enough fluids is because we don't have water with us. Keeping a bottle to hand will help keep you hydrated.

Acknowledgements

With many thanks to …
Gail Powell – Solopreneur Publishing
Muka Silver at Start Monday Snax
Lottie Ellen – Photography
Nadine McNulty - Food Stylist
Tahlia Jones-Bishop and Andre Watkins – Front Cover Photo
Colleen Robinson for the use of her beautiful house and kitchen.

How to Contact us ...

www.thefitnessfamily.uk
Jordan@thefitnessfamily.uk
Sophie@thefitnessfamily.uk

Instagram - jordanstorey90
Instagram - sophiewatkins7

Index

DINNERS